Scorpions

by Conrad J. Storad
photographs by Paula Jansen

Lerner Publications Company • Minneapolis, Minnesota

For my father and mother. You taught me that curiosity is the special key to understanding Nature's creatures, large and small.

—CJS

To Mom—Thanks for fostering and sharing an appreciation for life through books and living.

—PJ

Thanks to our series consultant, Sharyn Fenwick, elementary science/math specialist. Mrs. Fenwick was the winner of the National Science Teachers Association 1991 Distinguished Teaching Award. She also was the recipient of the Presidential Award for Excellence in Math and Science Teaching, representing the state of Minnesota at the elementary level in 1992. Thanks to Gary A. Polis for his assistance with the book. And special thanks to our young helper Ben Liestman.

The author and photographer would like to thank Neil Hadley, Ph.D., Arizona State University; and the Museum of Geology at Arizona State University for their assistance with this book. And special thanks to Marilyn Bloom "The Scorpion Lady," who runs the antivenin lab at ASU, for her patience and generosity of time and information.

Additional photographs are reproduced through the courtesy of: p. 29 Gary A. Polis; p. 35, © Robert and Linda Mitchell; pp. 36-37, 38, 39, 43, Graeme Lowe

Lerner Publications Company
A division of Lerner Publishing Group
241 First Avenue North
Minneapolis, MN 55401 U.S.A.

Website address: www.lernerbooks.com

Library of Congress Cataloging-in-Publication Data

Storad, Conrad J.
    Scorpions / by Conrad J. Storad ; photographs by Paula Jansen.
        p.   cm. — (Early bird nature books)
    Includes index.
    ISBN 0-8225-3004-X (lib. bdg. : alk. paper)
    1. Scorpions—Juvenile literature. [1. Scorpions.] I. Jansen,
Paula, ill. II. Title III. Series.
QL458.7.S76 1994
595.4'6—dc20   94-4634

Manufactured in the United States of America
3 4 5 6 7 8 – JR – 06 05 04 03 02 01

Contents

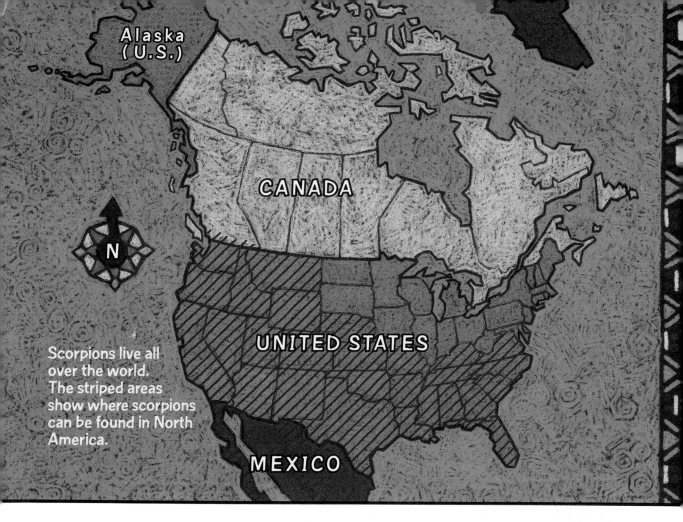

Alaska
(U.S.)

CANADA

N

Scorpions live all
over the world.
The striped areas
show where scorpions
can be found in North
America.

UNITED STATES

MEXICO

Be a Word Detective

Can you find these words as you read about the scorpion's life? Be a detective and try to figure out what they mean. You can turn to the glossary on page 47 for help.

abdomen	**cuticle**	**pincers**
antivenin	**exoskeleton**	**prosoma**
arachnids	**molting**	**telson**
brood	**nocturnal**	**venom**

Chapter 1

Scorpions looked like this hundreds of millions of years ago. Do you really know how long ago that was?

The World of Scorpions

Scorpions are scary-looking animals. They have been on earth longer than most animals alive today. The very first scorpions lived more than 450 million years ago. That's before dinosaurs were alive. But exactly how long ago was 450 million years? Pretend you are counting dollar bills. And pretend you count one dollar bill every second. It would take you more than 11 days to count to one million. To reach 450 million, you would have to count one dollar bill every second for more than 14 years!

Scorpions today look a lot like the scorpions of long ago, just a lot smaller.

Scorpions are related to spiders, ticks, mites, and other animals called arachnids (uh-RAK-nihdz). Scorpions also are related to shrimps and lobsters. In fact, without its curved tail, a scorpion looks a lot like a little lobster. But scorpions live on land, not in the ocean.

Lobsters are related to scorpions.

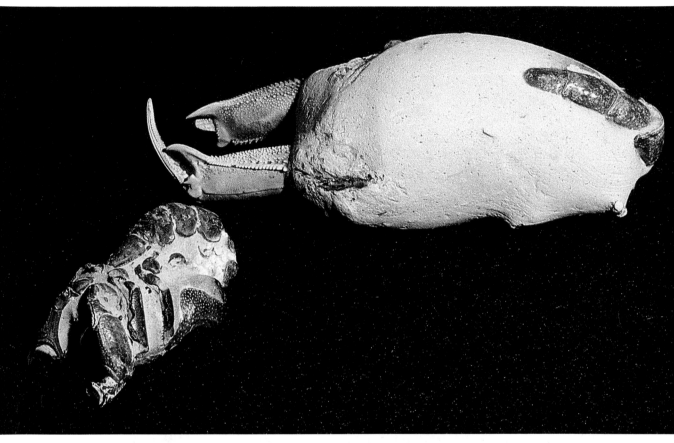

These are fossils of a scorpion (left) *and a crablike scorpion* (right) *that lived a long time ago. Like lobsters, crabs are related to scorpions.*

Long ago, scorpions did live in the ocean. They were some of the very first animals to crawl out of the ocean and live on land. Those old scorpions were 3 or 4 feet long, almost as big as your friends at school.

This scorpion can grow to be 4 inches long.

Luckily, scorpions living today are much smaller. They are usually only 1 or 2 inches long. The biggest scorpions are 8 inches long. That's about as long as a brand-new pencil.

Black emperor scorpions come from Africa. Some scorpions in Africa grow to be 8 inches long.

And they weigh almost as much as a hard-boiled egg. But these 8-inch-long scorpions are found only in the forests of the Ivory Coast. The Ivory Coast is a country in western Africa.

We know that 1,500 different kinds of scorpions live in the world today. There might be as many as 1,000 more to be discovered. Only 70–75 kinds of scorpions live in the United States.

This is the giant Arizona hairy scorpion. It is one of the many kinds of scorpions that live in the United States.

The giant Arizona hairy scorpion at left has the scientific name of Hadrurus arizonensis. *The bark scorpions below have the scientific name of* Centruroides sculpturatus.

Most scorpions live in deserts.

Scorpions are found in almost every place on earth. Some scorpions live in rocky and sandy deserts, while others like the wet soil of jungles. Some scorpions dig homes in grasslands, and some live in forests. Small, blind scorpions crawl around in caves far underground. Tiny scorpions live in the cracks of pineapples. One kind of scorpion lives high in the Himalaya Mountains. While no one has found scorpions in the icy cold of Antarctica, they could live there. Scorpions can live for a long time in very cold weather. They also can live for two days under water. But most scorpions live in deserts.

Some bark scorpions live in the cracks of palm trees.

Chapter 2

Scorpions can be different sizes and colors, but mainly they look very much the same. Can you tell how many legs scorpions have?

The Scorpion Sting

Like all arachnids, the scorpion's body is divided into two main parts. The front part is called the prosoma (proh-SOH-muh). The back part is called the abdomen. Scorpions have eight walking legs and two long claws called pincers (PIHN-serz). The scorpion's head, walking legs, and pincers are part of the prosoma. The most dangerous part of a scorpion is its long curved tail. The tail and stinger are on the abdomen.

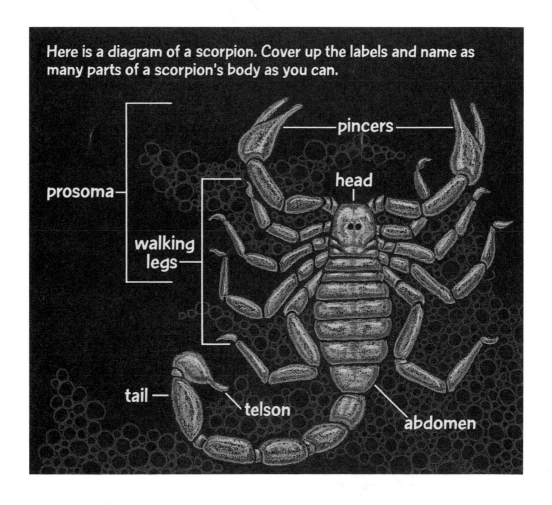

Here is a diagram of a scorpion. Cover up the labels and name as many parts of a scorpion's body as you can.

pincers

head

prosoma

walking legs

tail

telson

abdomen

Scorpions can move their tails from side to side and from back to front. But scorpions can't move their tails backward.

The scorpion's tail is both a weapon and a hunting tool. Scorpions use their tails to protect themselves from animals who like to eat them.

Scorpions also use their tails to hunt for the animals they eat. Inside the curved tail is a tiny sac. It is filled with a powerful poison called venom. At the tip of the tail is a stinger, called a telson. The telson injects venom into insects and other small animals. The venom makes it impossible for these small animals to move.

Scorpions catch crickets with their pincers before stinging them.

Only about 25 kinds of scorpions have venom strong enough to kill a person. About 5,000 people throughout the world die every year from scorpion stings. The sting of most scorpions is about as painful as the sting of a honeybee. It feels like a red-hot needle punched

This giant Arizona hairy scorpion is in attack position.

The sting of a bark scorpion can kill a person.

into your skin. The tiny bark scorpion is the only scorpion in the United States that has venom strong enough to kill a person. The bark scorpion lives in the Arizona desert. It is thin, less than 2 inches long, and the color of straw.

No one in the United States has died from a scorpion sting for almost 30 years. That's because people can get special medicine called antivenin (ant-ih-VEHN-ihn) from American hospitals. Antivenin includes a small amount of the scorpion's own poison. If you were stung by a scorpion, you would get an antivenin shot. The shot would help your body protect itself against the poison.

The blood from this goat helps make antivenin for scorpion stings.

Chapter 3

Scorpions can live for a long time. Do you know why?

Sticky Stew

Most scorpions live from 2 to 10 years. Some can live as long as 25 years. Scorpions live a long time because they use energy slowly.

Scorpions get energy from the food they eat. Sometimes it's hard for scorpions to find food. But they can live without food for up to a year. And some kinds of scorpions never need water. They get all the fluid they need from the bodies of the insects they eat. Using energy slowly helps scorpions live in the hot desert.

This scorpion will get energy from eating crickets.

The cuticle makes this scorpion look shiny.

Scorpions have a hard skin that feels like a fingernail. The hard skin is called an exoskeleton (ek-soh-SKEL-eh-ten). The exoskeleton is covered with a thin, waxy coat called cuticle (KYOO-teh-kuhl). The cuticle seals in all water. Scorpions don't sweat. Even water from their waste is saved. A scorpion's waste is nothing more than a pile of dry powder.

Scorpions, like this giant Arizona hairy scorpion, use the wind and nearby landmarks, like rocks and shrubs, to help them get around.

Scorpions are good hunters. They are nocturnal, sleeping during the day and hunting at night. Scientists think they use stars to see how to get from place to place. Invisible rays of light from the moon bounce off the scorpion's

This is what a giant Arizona hairy scorpion looks like to an insect.

hard exoskeleton. People can't see this kind of light, but insects can. Scorpions glow bright blue to green under these light rays. Some scientists think that scorpions glow to trick insects. The light makes insects come close to scorpions.

Scorpions have tiny slits on their legs that help them hunt. The slits help them feel sand move. Even when a beetle is walking a foot away, a scorpion can feel it.

Leg hairs help scorpions feel movement on the ground. The yellow part of the scorpion's abdomen also helps the scorpion feel. It sweeps the ground as the scorpion walks.

Scorpions eat other scorpions.

Scorpions are fierce hunters. They will attack anybody, including other scorpions. In fact, other than insects, a scorpion's favorite food is another scorpion.

Scorpions wait for their food to walk by.

A hungry scorpion will find a place on the ground or a tree to sit on. Then it waits. It stays perfectly still. A scorpion might wait for hours until an animal like a cricket comes close enough to touch. Then, faster than you can blink your eye, the scorpion grabs the cricket with its strong pincers. The scorpion holds on while its tail swoops down like a whip. The telson stings the unlucky cricket, again and again. The cricket can't move.

A scorpion catches a cricket with its pincers and stings the cricket with its tail.

Now the scorpion can take its time tearing the cricket into small pieces. The scorpion breaks each piece into tiny bits with its pincers and jaws. When the pile of bits is big enough, the scorpion spits strong juices from its mouth onto the pieces. The juices melt the pieces into a sticky stew. When the stew is gooey enough, the scorpion drinks until all of the cricket is gone.

A scorpion begins to eat a cricket.

Great horned owls like to eat scorpions.

Scorpions are not always the hunters. They spend lots of time hiding from animals who would like to eat them. The scorpion's telson keeps some hunters away. But many hunters put up with getting stung just to catch a tasty scorpion. Owls, bats, snakes, hawks, desert rats, and coyotes like to munch on scorpions if they can catch them.

Chapter 4

Scorpions are usually alone, but two will get together when it's time to have a family. How many babies do you think a scorpion can have at one time?

A Family Ride

Scorpions don't lay eggs like other arachnids. They give birth to live young. A scorpion may have from 1 to 105 babies in

34

a single brood. A brood is the scorpion family. It is all the babies born at the same time. Once born, the babies crawl onto their mother's back. The mother scorpion does not feed the babies while they ride on her back. But she does protect them.

Babies ride on their mother's back for about two weeks.

When other food is hard to find, mother scorpions often eat their own babies. This is not as horrible as it sounds. If little food can be found, the baby scorpions and the mother would starve and die. Instead, the babies are

Sometimes, mother scorpions eat their babies.

food for the mother. They keep her alive long enough for her to have another brood. And the new batch of babies might have a better chance of living.

Mother scorpions don't always eat their babies. In fact, they often protect them from danger. Baby scorpions are safe riding on their mother's back. They are safe beneath her curved tail. Other scorpions would love to eat the tiny babies but don't want to get the mother angry. They don't want to be stung.

The babies are safe under their mother's tail.

This scorpion is molting. The old skin is yellow compared to the new skin.

Baby scorpions live on their mother's back for almost two weeks. After two weeks, they are living on their own. Then young scorpions grow until they get too big for their own skin. They break out of the old skin. This is called molting.

Scorpions molt many times before they become adults. They can take seven years to become fully grown.

When the babies are gone, mother scorpions continue to sleep in holes under rocks or under loose tree bark during the day. They

After their babies are gone, mother scorpions continue doing scorpion things.

Mother scorpions may start another family after one
brood has left.

*After their babies are gone, mother scorpions continue
to hunt at night.*

continue to hunt for insects and spiders and
other scorpions at night. Scorpions have been
around for a very long time. They know how to
survive. Scorpions probably will be living on
earth for a long, long time to come.

On Sharing a Book

As you know, adults greatly influence a child's attitude toward reading. When a child sees you read, or when you share a book with a child, you're sending a message that reading is important. Show your child that reading a book together is important to you. Find a comfortable, quiet place. Turn off the television and limit other distractions like telephone calls.

Be prepared to start slowly. Take turns reading parts of this book. Stop and talk about what you're reading. Talk about the photographs. You may find that much of the shared time is spent discussing just a few pages. This discussion time is valuable for both of you, so don't move through the book too quickly. If your child begins to lose interest, stop reading. Continue sharing the book at another time. When you do pick up the book again, be sure to revisit the parts you have already read. Most importantly, enjoy the book!

Be a Vocabulary Detective

You will find a word list on page 5. Words selected for this list are important to the understanding of the topic of this book. Encourage your child to be a word detective and search for the words as you read the book together. Talk about what the words mean and how they are used in the sentence. Do any of these words have more than one meaning? You will find these words defined in a glossary on page 47.

What about Questions?

Use questions to make sure your child understands the information in this book. Here are some suggestions:

> What did this paragraph tell us? What does this picture show? What do you think we'll learn about next? What animals are related to scorpions? How do scorpions defend themselves? Do scorpions live in your state? Scorpions are often thought of as villains. What are some of a scorpion's good characteristics? What is your favorite part in the book?

If your child has questions, don't hesitate to respond with questions of your own like: What do *you* think? Why? What is it that you don't know? If your child can't remember certain facts, turn to the index.

Introducing the Index

The index is an important learning tool. It helps readers get information quickly without searching throughout the whole book. Turn to the index on page 48. Choose an entry, such as *tail*, and ask your child to use the index to find out how scorpions use their tails. Repeat this exercise with as many entries as you like. Ask your child to point out the differences between an index and a glossary. (The glossary tells readers what words mean, while the index helps readers find information quickly.)

Where in the World?

Many plants and animals found in the Early Bird Nature Books series live in parts of the world other than the United States. Encourage your child to find the places mentioned in this book on a world map or globe. Take time to talk about climate, terrain, and how your family might live in such places.

All the World in Metric!

Although our monetary system is in metric units (based on multiples of 10), the United States is one of the few countries in the world that does not use the metric system of measurement. Here are some conversion activities you and your child can do using a calculator:

WHEN YOU KNOW:	MULTIPLY BY:	TO FIND:
miles	1.609	kilometers
feet	0.3048	meters
inches	2.54	centimeters
gallons	3.787	liters
tons	0.907	metric tons
pounds	0.454	kilograms

Family Activities

Visit a zoo or pet shop to observe a living scorpion. What is its environment like? Why?

Make a model of a scorpion out of clay or Play-Doh. Think about the scorpion's environment and build a scene around your scorpion model using items found in your backyard.

Glossary

abdomen—the back part of the scorpion's body

antivenin (ant-ih-VEHN-ihn)—medicine that protects people from an animal's poisonous bite

arachnids (uh-RAK-nihdz)—members of a group of animals with eight legs. Scorpions, mites, and ticks are among the animals in this group.

brood—a group of babies born at the same time in the same family

cuticle (KYOO-teh-kuhl)—the thin, waxy coat of a scorpion

exoskeleton (ek-soh-SKEL-eh-ten)—the scorpion's hard, protective covering

molting—getting rid of the old exoskeleton to make way for a new one

nocturnal—active at night

pincers (PIHN-serz)—claws

prosoma (proh-SOH-muh)—the front part of the scorpion's body, which includes the head, eight walking legs, and two pincers

telson—the stinger at the tip of the scorpion's tail

venom—poison

Index